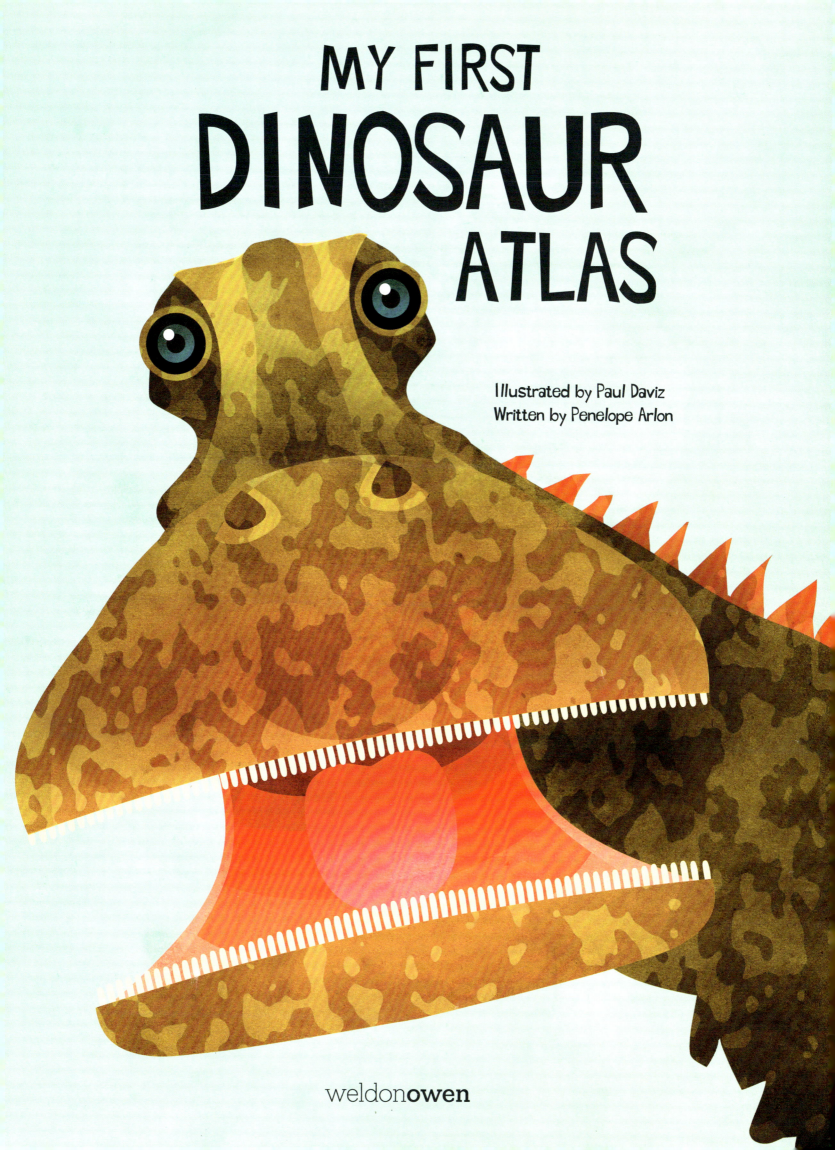

MY FIRST DINOSAUR ATLAS

Illustrated by Paul Daviz
Written by Penelope Arlon

weldon**owen**

Illustrated by Paul Daviz

Written by Penelope Arlon

Palaeontologist Consultant – Dr. Neil Clark,
The Hunterian Museum

Published by Weldon Owen Children's Books
An imprint of Weldon Owen International, L.P.
A subsidiary of Insight International, L.P.
PO Box 3088
San Rafael, CA 94912
www.insighteditions.com

Weldon Owen Children's Books
Editor: Stella Caldwell
Designer: Tory Gordon-Harris
Senior Production Manager: Greg Steffen
Art Director: Stuart Smith
Publisher: Sue Grabham

Insight Editions
Publisher: Raoul Goff

A CIP catalogue record for this book is available from the British Library.

ISBN: 9781681889740

Manufactured, printed, and assembled in China.
First printing 2022 DRM0622
26 25 24 23 22 5 4 3 2 1

MIX
Paper from
responsible sources
FSC® C169965

CONTENTS

A WORLD OF DINOSAURS

Once upon a time, millions of years ago, all kinds of dinosaurs wandered the Earth. Gigantic plant-eaters shook the ground as they walked. Ferocious meat-eaters hunted with deadly teeth and sharp claws. Some dinosaurs had feathers. Others had amazing horns, spikes, frills or crests.

Many other kinds of animals lived in dinosaur times too. Strange creatures flew through the skies and huge reptiles hunted in the seas. But the amazing dinosaurs ruled the land. In fact, they lived on Earth for 165 million years. Are you ready to meet them?

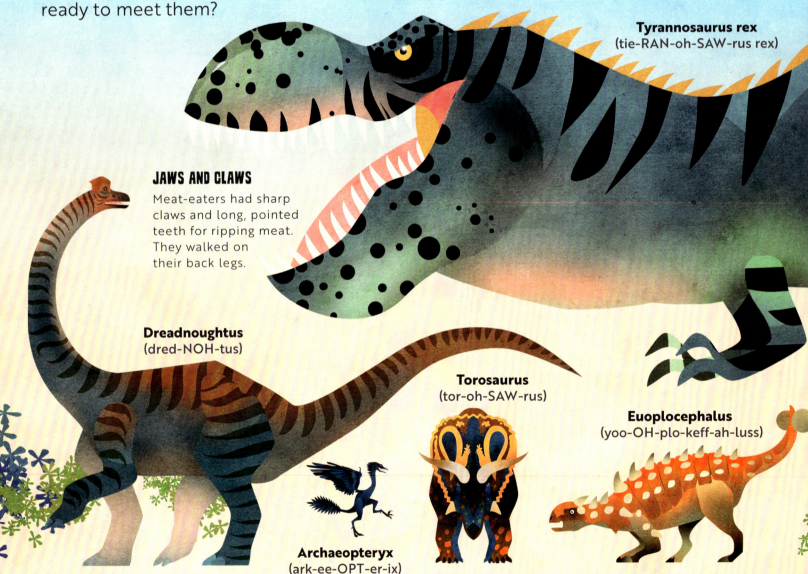

Dimorphodon
(die-MORE-foh-don)

Tyrannosaurus rex
(tie-RAN-oh-SAW-rus rex)

JAWS AND CLAWS
Meat-eaters had sharp claws and long, pointed teeth for ripping meat. They walked on their back legs.

Dreadnoughtus
(dred-NOH-tus)

Torosaurus
(tor-oh-SAW-rus)

Euoplocephalus
(yoo-OH-plo-keff-ah-luss)

Archaeopteryx
(ark-ee-OPT-er-ix)

GIGANTIC DINOSAURS
Huge, plant-munching dinosaurs had small heads, and long necks and tails. Some were as big as three double-decker buses.

MINI DINOSAURS
The smallest dinosaurs were the size of a chicken. Many were covered in feathers like a bird.

DECORATED DINOSAURS
Some dinosaurs had spikes, crests or other amazing features. The huge frill on this dinosaur helped it to find a mate.

ARMOURED DINOSAURS
The tough, spiky skin of some dinosaurs was like armour. It protected them from the dangerous teeth and claws of hungry meat-eaters.

SPOT IT! Roar around the world to spot the biggest, smallest, fiercest, spikiest

SKY SWOOPERS

The skies were filled with flying reptiles called pterosaurs. Some of them were as big as small aeroplanes!

and most awesome dinosaurs. Which is your favourite?

Peteinosaurus
(pe-TINE-o-SAW-rus)

Mussaurus
(moo-SAW-rus)

BAT WINGS

Peteinosaurus was the size of a large bat. This pterosaur had a long tail, leathery wings and narrow jaws full of sharp, pointed teeth.

Coelophysis
(seel-OH-fie-sis)

FAST RUNNER

Eoraptor was fox-sized. It caught small lizards to eat with its sharp teeth and claws.

Eoraptor
(EE-oh-RAP-tor)

SPOT IT! How many swooping pterosaurs can you spot?

LEAF CHOMPER

Riojasaurus spent most of its time chewing leaves with its spoon-shaped teeth. Its long, bendy neck helped it to reach high up into the trees.

Riojasaurus
(ree-oh-hah-SAW-rus)

Liliensternus
(lil-ee-en-shtern-us)

Coloradisaurus
(ko-lo-rahd-i-SAW-rus)

THE TRIASSIC

The first dinosaurs lived in a time called the Triassic (try-ass-ik). It was a very different world from today. There were no people, houses, cities or countries – just one huge island surrounded by a great blue ocean.

The land was hot, dry and dusty. But it was cooler by the sea, where trees and ferns grew, and where most of the dinosaurs lived. Many Triassic dinosaurs were small, speedy meat-eaters like *Eoraptor* or *Coelophysis*. They ran on two legs looking for small animals and insects to eat.

Staurikosaurus
(stor-ik-oh-SAW-rus)

Nyasasaurus
(nye-as-a-SAW-rus)

THE TRIASSIC (252–201 MYA)
At the beginning of Triassic times. . .
. . . the world looked like this!

Which Triassic dinosaurs have long necks?

JURASSIC GIANTS

In Jurassic (juh-rass-ik) times it was warm and there was plenty of rain. Thick, damp forests covered the land, and lush, green plants grew alongside the rivers and beneath the tall trees. There was lots of food for the animals to eat.

Many different kinds of dinosaurs roamed the world and some of them grew to incredible sizes. Long-necked plant-eaters munched from the highest branches, and hungry meat-eaters prowled the forests. The dinosaurs were the biggest, fiercest and fastest creatures on Earth.

Allosaurus
(AL-oh-SAW-rus)

TERRIFYING HUNTER

Fierce *Allosaurus* was one of the biggest meat-eaters of the Jurassic. It ripped its food apart with enormous, pointed teeth.

Ceratosaurus
(keh-RAT-oh-SAW-rus)

Heterodontosaurus
(HET-er-oh-DONT-oh-SAW-rus)

SPOT IT! Look at *Giraffatitan*'s neck. Can you guess how this dinosaur got its name?

Dimorphodon
(die-MORE-foh-don)

Diplodocus
(DIP-low-DOCK-us)

SPIKY FIGHTER
Stegosaurus used its spiked tail to fight off enemies like *Allosaurus*. The huge plates on its back made it look big and scary.

Giraffatitan
(ji-raf-a-tie-tan)

Stegosaurus
(STEG-oh-SAW-rus)

Compsognathus
(komp-sog-NATH-us)

MIGHTY MUNCHER
Leaf-eating *Apatosaurus* was the length of two school buses. It could whip attackers with its long, powerful tail.

THE JURASSIC (201–145 MYA)
In the middle of Jurassic times. . .

Apatosaurus
(ah-PAT-oh-SAW-rus)

Archaeopteryx
(ark-ee-OPT-er-ix)

. . .the world looked like this!

What kinds of tails can you spot?

BIG BITER

Dangerous *Giganotosaurus* hunted other large dinosaurs. Its gigantic jaws were packed with teeth like knives.

Giganotosaurus
(gig-an-OH-toe-SAW-rus)

Styracosaurus
(sty-RAK-oh-SAW-rus)

Struthiomimus
(STROOTH-ee-oh-MEEM-us)

Ankylosaurus
(an-KIE-loh-SAW-rus)

QUICK RUNNER

Feathered *Struthiomimus* looked a bit like an ostrich. It could run fast on its long legs to escape hungry meat-eaters.

Torosaurus
(tor-oh-SAW-rus)

THE CRAZY CRETACEOUS

In the Cretaceous (kri-TEY-shuhs), the world looked almost the same as today. There were forests, swamps and open plains with grass. Flowers dotted the land, and bees and other insects buzzed through the air.

Crazy-looking dinosaurs of all shapes and sizes roamed the world. Some were covered with long feathers, and some had impressive crests. There were dinosaurs with thick, bony heads, and others with awesome spikes and horns.

Deinonychus
(die-NON-i-kuss)shun)

SPOT IT! How many dinosaurs can you see with feathers?

Oviraptor
(OH-vee-RAP-tor)

Amargasaurus
(a-MARG-ah-SAW-rus)

Parasaurolophus
(pa-ra-saw-ro-LOAF-us)

Therizinosaurus
(THER-ih-zin-oh-SAW-rus)

CRAZY CLAWS

Therizinosaurus was the dinosaur with the longest claws!

SPECIAL SPIKES

The six long spikes around the head of *Styracosaurus* made this dinosaur look strong. They helped it to find a mate.

Pachycephalosaurus
(pack-i-keff-ah-loh-SAW-rus)

Unenlagia
(oon-en-lahg-ee-ah)

THE CRETACEOUS (145–66 MYA)

Towards the end of Cretaceous times...

...the world looked like this!

Which dinosaur has a long, pointed horn on its nose?

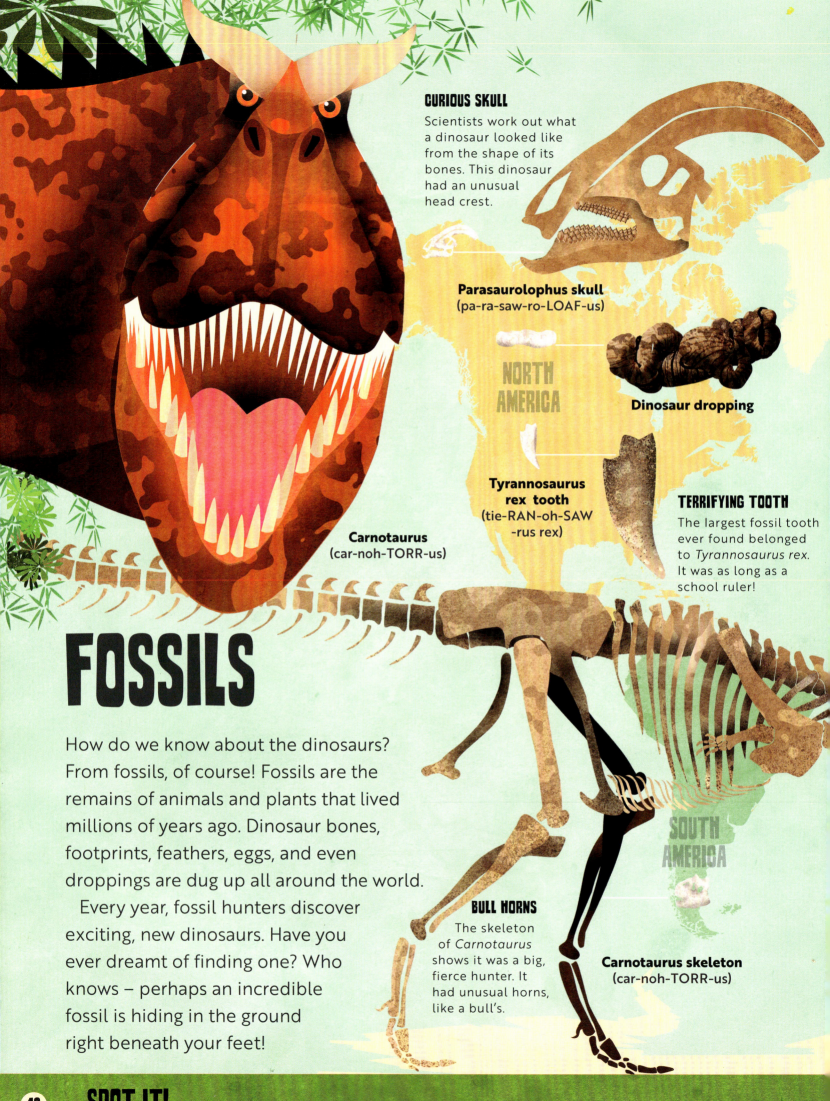

CURIOUS SKULL

Scientists work out what a dinosaur looked like from the shape of its bones. This dinosaur had an unusual head crest.

Parasaurolophus skull
(pa-ra-saw-ro-LOAF-us)

NORTH AMERICA

Dinosaur dropping

Tyrannosaurus rex tooth
(tie-RAN-oh-SAW -rus rex)

TERRIFYING TOOTH

The largest fossil tooth ever found belonged to *Tyrannosaurus rex*. It was as long as a school ruler!

Carnotaurus
(car-noh-TORR-us)

FOSSILS

How do we know about the dinosaurs? From fossils, of course! Fossils are the remains of animals and plants that lived millions of years ago. Dinosaur bones, footprints, feathers, eggs, and even droppings are dug up all around the world.

Every year, fossil hunters discover exciting, new dinosaurs. Have you ever dreamt of finding one? Who knows – perhaps an incredible fossil is hiding in the ground right beneath your feet!

BULL HORNS

The skeleton of *Carnotaurus* shows it was a big, fierce hunter. It had unusual horns, like a bull's.

SOUTH AMERICA

Carnotaurus skeleton
(car-noh-TORR-us)

SPOT IT! What kinds of fossils can you see? Have you ever found a fossil?

Large plant-eater's leg bone

FIERCE FIGHT

An amazing fossil was found of these two dinosaurs together. It shows they were fighting when they died.

Protoceratops and Velociraptor fossil
(pro-toe-SER-ah-tops)
(vel-OSS-ee-RAP-tor)

Therizinosaurus claw
(THER-ih-zin-oh-SAW-rus)

Sciurumimus feather
(skee-ORE-ooh-MEEM-us)

EUROPE

ASIA

AFRICA

STEP BY STEP

Sometimes, lots of dinosaur footprints are found together in one place. This shows that some dinosaurs lived in herds.

Spinosaurus skull
(SPINE-oh-SAW-rus)

AMAZING EGGS

All dinosaurs laid eggs. Some were long and oval, and some were round like tennis balls.

AUSTRALASIA

Dinosaur footprints

Massospondylus eggs
(mass-oh-SPON-di-luss)

Massospondylus

ANTARCTICA

NORTH AMERICA

Have you ever visited North America? Or perhaps you live there? There are lots of incredible fossils buried in North America's deserts, canyons and mountains. Dinosaur hunters have found spikes, horns, frills, claws and jaws full of sharp teeth. Can you see some of these things on the dinosaurs on the map?

Tyrannosaurus rex, or *T. rex*, is probably the most famous dinosaur of all. Did you know this mighty meat-eater once roamed across North America? It was fierce enough to kill any dinosaur it met!

TOOTING TRUMPET

Scientists think that *Parasaurolophus* used the large crest on its head to make loud honking calls.

toot-toot! HONK

Parasaurolophus
(pa-ra-saw-ro-LOAF-us)

BONE CRUNCHER

The powerful jaws of *Tyrannosaurus rex* could stretch wide open. Its huge, pointed teeth were strong enough to crush bones.

Troodon
(TROH-oh-don)

Tyrannosaurus rex
(tie-RAN-oh-SAW-rus rex)

Utahraptor
(YOO-tah-RAP-tor)

Lambeosaurus
(lam-BEE-oh-SAW-rus)

SPOT IT! Do you see any spikes?

TERRIBLE TAIL

Euoplocephalus had a huge club at the end of its tail. It could strike the legs of deadly hunters such as *Tyrannosaurus rex*.

Euoplocephalus
(yoo-OH-plo-keff-ah-luss)

Plateosaurus
(plat-ee-oh-SAW-rus)

Borealopelta
(BOH-ree-AH-low-PELL-ta)

Corythosaurus
(koh-rith-oh-SAW-rus)

Maiasaura
(my-ah-SORE-ah)

Anzu
(AHN-zoo)

Torosaurus
(tor-oh-SAW-rus)

CLAWED HANDS

Plateosaurus walked on its back legs and used its hands to gather leaves from trees.

Triceratops
(try-SER-ah-tops)

Dracorex hogwartsia
(DRAK-oh-rex hog-wart-see-ah)

Pentaceratops
(pent-ah-SER-ah-tops)

ENORMOUS EGGS

The fossil eggs of *Apatosaurus* are the size of footballs!

Apatosaurus
(ah-PAT-oh-SAW-rus)

How many dinosaurs can you see with horns on their heads?

15

SOUTH AMERICA

Some of the biggest dinosaurs ever discovered once lived in South America. One of them is *Dreadnoughtus*. Fossil scientists think this mighty leaf-muncher weighed as much as eight African elephants!

Many other huge dinosaurs roamed this part of the world. Enormous plant-eaters ate from the tallest trees. Massive meat-eaters chased after other dinosaurs. Hefty dinosaurs, with beaks like a duck's, lived together in large herds. South America really was the land of giants!

Dreadnoughtus

STOMPING LEGS
The front legs of *Dreadnoughtus* were as high as two people standing one on top of the other.

SPOT IT! How many dinosaurs can you see that walk on four legs?

Tachiraptor
(tah-chee-RAP-tor)

Laquintasaura
(la-KWIN-tuh-SORE-ah)

HERD SAFETY
Laquintasaura was the size of a small dog. It lived in herds to keep safe.

Padillasaurus
(pah-DILL-a-SAW-rus)

Yamanasaurus
(yah-MAN-ah-SAW-rus)

Irritator
(irr-it-ate-or)

SNAPPING JAWS
Irritator had long, narrow jaws, like a crocodile's. It mostly ate fish.

Saltasaurus
(salt-ah-SAW-rus)

Antarctosaurus
(ant-ARK-toe-SAW-rus)

Vespersaurus
(VES-per-SAW-rus)

Eoraptor
(EE-oh-RAP-tor)

Staurikosaurus
(stor-ik-oh-SAW-rus)

Guaibasaurus
(gwie-bah-SAW-rus)

Amargasaurus

Herrerasaurus
(herr-ray-rah-SAW-rus)

Amargasaurus
(a-MARG-ah-SAW-rus)

NOISY RATTLE
Amargasaurus had a double row of spines running along its neck and back. Perhaps it rattled them to scare away big meat-eaters.

Lapampasaurus
(la-pam-pah-SAW-rus)

Dreadnoughtus
(dred-NOH-tus)

Carnotaurus
(car-noh-TORR-us)

CHAMPION RUNNER
Carnotaurus had long, slim legs and a thick, muscly tail. They helped this meat-eater to run fast after its prey.

Can you see a dinosaur with a knobbly, bumpy back?

EUROPE

Did you know Europe is where the very first dinosaur fossil was discovered? The dinosaur was named *Megalosaurus*. Since then, amazing fossils of every shape and size have been dug up. Many big dinosaurs lived in Europe, but there were plenty of small ones, too. *Compsognathus* was the size of a chicken.

This tiny terror was a fierce and fast hunter! Some amazing feathered dinosaurs have been discovered in Europe. One of them is *Sciurumimus*. This fluffy meat-eater had a big, bushy tail like a squirrel's.

HUNGRY HUNTER

Megalosaurus was a fierce meat-eater. This killer's teeth were like sharp blades.

Saltopus
(sal-to-pus)

Megalosaurus
(MEG-ah-low-SAW-rus)

Scelidosaurus
(skel-EYE-doh-SAW-rus)

Dacentrurus

DANGEROUS SPIKES

Dacentrurus had big plates running down its back. A spiky tail helped to keep its enemies away.

Dacentrurus
(dah-sen-troo-russ)

Torvosaurus
(TOR-voh-SAW-rus)

SPOT IT! Can you see a herd of small dinosaurs?

THUMB SPIKE

Look at the big spike on *Iguanodon*'s thumb! It could have been used to poke attackers, or it might have been used to gather tough leaves.

Plateosaurus
(plat-ee-oh-SAW-rus)

Iguanodon

Iguanodon
(ig-WHA-noh-don)

Europasaurus
(yoo-roh-pah-SAW-rus)

Burianosaurus
(boo-ree-AN-oh-SAW-rus)

Sciurumimus
(skee-ORE-ooh-MEEM-us)

Struthiosaurus
(STROOTH-ee-oh-SAW-rus)

Balaur
(bal-or)

Magyarosaurus
(mag-yar-oh-SAW-rus)

Compsognathus
(komp-sog-NATH-us)

Tethyshadros
(tee-thiss-HAD-ros)

HUGE EGGS

The first fossil dinosaur eggs ever found belonged to *Hypselosaurus*. This big dinosaur buried its eggs in a shallow hole in the ground.

Hypselosaurus
(hip-sel-oh-SAW-rus)

Which is the dinosaur with a thumb spike?

IN THE SKIES AND SEAS

Imagine looking up in dinosaur times to see an enormous flying creature. The pterosaurs were winged reptiles that came in many different sizes. *Eudimorphodon* was no bigger than a crow, but *Hatzegopteryx* was the size of a small plane!

Deep in the oceans, gigantic reptiles hunted their prey. Fast-swimming *Liopleurodon* silently cruised through the water. Terrifying *Mosasaurus* attacked other reptiles with huge, deadly jaws.

Dimorphodon
(die-MORE-foh-don)

Pterodactylus
(tear-uh-DACK-til-us)

Liopleurodon (lie-oh-PLUR-oh-don)

FLAPPING FLIPPERS

Liopleurodon was the size of a killer whale. It swam by beating its flippers up and down.

Pliosaur
(ply-oh-sore)

Stenopterygius
(sten-op-ter-IH-jee-us)

SPOT IT! Can you find a pterosaur with sharp, pointed teeth?

Eudimorphodon
(yoo-dye-MORF-oh-don)

WINGED TERROR
Hatzegopteryx was one of the largest pterosaurs that ever lived. It probably feasted on baby dinosaurs.

Hatzegopteryx
(hat-seh-GOP-ter-ix)

Bakonydraco
(bay-kon-EYE-dray-coe)

TOOTHY HUNTER
The long jaws of *Rhamphorhynchus* were full of needle-sharp teeth. It fed on fish and insects.

Rhamphorhynchus
(ram-for-HIN-kus)

Shonisaurus
(show-nee-SAW-rus)

Mosasaurus
(moh-zuh-SAW-rus)

Nothosaurus
(not-oh-SAW-rus)

SEA AND SHORE
Nothosaurus hunted for fish in the sea. It had four short legs, and could come out of the water to rest on the shore.

Which sea reptile could walk on land?

AFRICA

Have you ever heard of *Spinosaurus*? This gigantic fish-eating dinosaur was discovered in Africa. In fact, it is the biggest flesh-eating dinosaur ever found! Can you imagine it wading through a steamy swamp and snapping its long crocodile jaws? Toothy *Nigersaurus* is another awesome dinosaur from this part of the world. This bulky plant-eater had more than five hundred teeth packed into its wide mouth.

Fossil hunters discovered the oldest dinosaur eggs ever found in Africa. They belonged to a long-necked plant-eater called *Massospondylus*. Some of the eggs still had tiny baby dinosaurs inside them.

Atlasaurus
(at-la-SAW-rus)

Cetiosaurus
(see-TEE-oh-SAW-rus)

SHARK TEETH
Carcharodontosaurus had long, jagged teeth like a shark's. It used them to pierce and tear apart meat.

Carcharodontosaurus
(kar-KAR-o-don-toe-SAW-rus)

BABY DINOSAURS
Massospondylus laid its eggs in a nest in the ground. After the babies hatched, they grew very fast to reach the size of their parents.

Massospondylus

SPOT IT! Which dinosaur has a very spiky tail?

Bahariasaurus
(buh-HAR-ree-uh-SAW-rus)

Nigersaurus

Spinosaurus
(SPINE-oh-SAW-rus)

Ouranosaurus
(oo-RAH-noh-SAW-rus)

Nigersaurus
(nee-zhayr-SAW-rus)

Suchomimus
(sook-oh-MEEM-us)

MOTOR MOUTH

Plant-eating *Nigersaurus* never stopped munching. Each of its 500 teeth was replaced every two weeks!

Kentrosaurus
(ken-troh-SAW-rus)

Elaphrosaurus
(el-a-fro-SAW-rus)

Malawisaurus
(mah-lah-wee-SAW-rus)

Massospondylus
(mass-oh-SPON-di-luss)

Majungasaurus
(mah-JUNG-gah-SAW-rus)

Pegomastax
(peg-oh-MAS-tax)

Heterodontosaurus
(HET-er-oh-DONT-oh-SAW-rus)

Nqwebasaurus
(n-qu-web-ah-SAW-rus)

Coelophysis
(seel-OH-fie-sis)

Rapetosaurus
(rah-PAY-to-SAW-rus)

Can you see a dinosaur with a sail on its back?

ASIA

There were many unusual dinosaurs in the world, but one plant-eater from Asia really was an oddball. Tall *Therizinosaurus* had a long neck, a small beaked head, and a great, round belly. Its enormous claws were as long as baseball bats!

Many feathered dinosaurs have been discovered in Asia. Little meat-eating *Microraptor* had long feathers on its arms and legs, but it couldn't fly. Fierce *Yutyrannus* was a feathery giant that may have hunted in packs.

Sibirotitan
(si-bi-ro-tie-tan)

FOSSIL FINDS
Many dinosaur fossils have been found in Asia's Gobi Desert.

Jaxartosaurus
(jak-sahr-toh-SAW-rus)

QUICK MOVER
Urbacodon was a speedy little hunter. Its big eyes and sharp hearing helped it to find small animals to eat.

Urbacodon
(urb-ah-ko-don)

Yutyrannus
(yoo-ti-RAN-us)

Isisaurus
(iss-ee-SAW-rus)

GROUND SHAKER
This hefty giant had a very thick neck. *Isisaurus* lived in herds to keep safe from hungry meat-eaters.

SPOT IT! Can you see a dinosaur with a very thick neck?

Mamenchisaurus

Therizinosaurus
(THER-ih-zin-oh-SAW-rus)

Citipati
(chit-i-puh-tih)

Microraptor
(MIKE-row-RAP-tor)

Micropachycephalosaurus
(MIKE-row-pak-ee-keff-ah-loh-SAW-rus)

PRIZE NECK
Mamenchisaurus had the longest neck of any dinosaur. It was as long as five giraffe necks!

Confuciusornis
(kon-few-shus-or-niss)

Koshisaurus
(koh-shee-SAW-rus)

Fukuivenator
(foo-KOO-ee-veh-nah-tor)

Tuojiangosaurus
(too-YANG-oh-SAW-rus)

Mamenchisaurus
(mah-men-chi-SAW-rus)

Isanosaurus
(ee-SAH-no-SAW-rus)

Which small dinosaur has a long name beginning with M? Can you say it?

THE GOBI

Today, the Gobi is a huge desert in the middle of Asia. It is a vast, dry wilderness. But it was very different in dinosaur times. There were lush, green forests, and rivers and streams criss-crossed the land. It was the perfect place for dinosaurs to live.

Can you imagine a pack of *Velociraptors* chasing their prey? These vicious hunters had savage teeth and claws. Long-legged *Gallimimus* sprinted across the land to escape danger. It was the fastest dinosaur of all.

NUT CRACKER
Psittacosaurus used its parrot-like beak to gather seeds and crack nuts. It had sharp teeth to cut its food.

Psittacosaurus
(SIT-ak-oh-SAW-rus)

Deinocheirus
(DINE-oh-KIRE-us)

Prenocephale
(preen-oh-keff-ah-lee)

Velociraptor
(vel-OSS-ee-RAP-tor)

KILLER CLAWS
Velociraptor had a huge, hooked claw on the second toe of each foot. It was used to slash and kill prey.

SPOT IT! Which dinosaur is looking after its eggs?

DEADLY GIANT

Tarbosaurus had around sixty teeth in its massive jaws. It could grip struggling animals with its clawed hands.

Tarbosaurus
(TAR-bow-SAW-rus)

Oviraptor
(OH-vee-RAP-tor)

CARING PARENT

Oviraptor looked after its eggs like birds do today. It sat on its nest to keep the eggs warm, and to protect them from danger.

Gallimimus
(gal-ee-MEEM-us)

Protoceratops
(pro-toe-SER-ah-tops)

THE GOBI

Today, the Gobi is a huge desert in China and Mongolia.

Can you see a dinosaur with a bony, dome-shaped head?

Austrosaurus

snort—snort
snuffle

NOISY NOSE
Look at the bump
on this dinosaur's
snout. Perhaps
Muttaburrasaurus
made loud sounds
with it.

OCEANIA

Only a few dinosaurs have been unearthed in this part
of the world, but all kinds of amazing footprints have
been discovered. In fact, the world's biggest dinosaur
tracks were found here.

Australia's most famous dinosaur is
Muttaburrasaurus. This big-nosed
leaf-muncher could stand up on
its back legs to eat from the
tall trees.

Muttaburrasaurus
(MUT-a-BURR-a-SAW-rus)

BIG EATER
Austrosaurus
was about the
length of five
cars. It spent its
time gathering
leaves from
the treetops.

Austrosaurus
(aws-troh-SAW-rus)

Minmi
(min-mee)

Rhoetosaurus
(reet-oh-SAW-rus)

Ozraptor
(oz-RAP-tor)

Weewarrasaurus
(wee-warr-a-SAW-rus)

Atlascopcosaurus
(at-la-SKOP-ko-SAW-rus)

Leaellynasaura
(lee-ELL-in-a-SORE-ah)

SPOT IT! Which dinosaur has a long, feathered tail?

ANTARCTICA

Today, icy Antarctica is the coldest place on Earth, but it was much warmer in dinosaur times. All sorts of creatures once lived in its lush forests.

Crested *Cryolophosaurus* was king of the meat-eaters. Perhaps you can imagine this fearsome hunter using its huge jaws and claws to attack a plant-eater like *Glacialisaurus*?

COLOURFUL CROWN

Cryolophosaurus had a curly crest on top of its head. It might have helped this meat-eater to find a mate.

Morrosaurus
(moe-row-SAW-rus)

Cryolophosaurus
(cry-o-LOAF-oh-SAW-rus)

Trinisaura
(trin-a-SORE-ah)

Glacialisaurus
(glay-see-al-ee-SAW-rus)

Antarctopelta
(ant-ARK-toe-PELL-ta)

FROZEN FOSSIL

Antarctopelta was a stocky plant-eater covered in bony plates. It took fossil hunters ten years to dig its bones out of the frozen ground.

SPOT IT! Can you see any dinosaurs with plates of armour?

A–Z OF DINOSAURS

SPOT IT!   How many dinosaurs' names begin with the letter 'D'?

Can you find 'Jaxartosaurus'? Which page is it on?

SPOT IT! How do you say 'Struthiomimus'?